CELEBRATING THE CITY OF JEJU

Celebrating the City of Jeju

Walter the Educator

Silent King Books

Copyright © 2024 by Walter the Educator

All rights reserved. No part of this book may be reproduced in any manner whatsoever without written per- mission except in the case of brief quotations embodied in critical articles and reviews.

First Printing, 2024

Disclaimer

This book is a literary work; the story is not about specific persons, locations, situations, and/or circumstances unless mentioned in a historical context. Any resemblance to real persons, locations, situations, and/or circumstances is coincidental. This book is for entertainment and informational purposes only. The author and publisher offer this information without warranties expressed or implied. No matter the grounds, neither the author nor the publisher will be accountable for any losses, injuries, or other damages caused by the reader's use of this book. The use of this book acknowledges an understanding and acceptance of this disclaimer.

Celebrating the City of Jeju is a little collectible souvenir book that belongs to the Celebrating Cities Book Series by Walter the Educator. Collect them all and more books at WaltertheEducator.com

USE THE EXTRA SPACE TO TAKE NOTES AND DOCUMENT YOUR MEMORIES

JEJU

Jeju, where the waves waltz with the winds,

Celebrating the City of Jeju

Of time, where every story begins.

Island of mysteries, cloaked in volcanic grace,

A symphony of whispers, nature's gentle embrace.

Halla-san's peak, a sentinel so grand,

Guarding the secrets of this enchanted land.

Ancient trails where footsteps merge with lore,

Echoes of pilgrims who wandered here before.

Seogwipo's shores, where ocean's breath does sigh,

Kissing the cliffs where dreams take to the sky.

Waterfalls cascading, laughter in their song,

In Jeju's heart, we find where we belong.

Tangerine groves, golden in the sun's embrace,

Fruit of the earth, a sweet and tender trace.

Farmers' hands, weathered yet so proud,

Harvesting the bounty, beneath the sky's vast shroud.

Celebrating the City of
Jeju

Haenyeo dive, fearless in the sea's cool grasp,

Their legacy of courage, in every breath they gasp.

Mothers of the deep, daughters of the tide,

In Jeju's waters, where legends still abide.

Jeju stone walls, whispers of the past,

Crafted by hands, enduring and steadfast.

Labyrinths of memory, leading hearts to roam,

In every path, a promise of coming home.

Cherry blossoms bloom, a fleeting pink delight,

Stars in the day, before they fade to night.

Their petals dance, on winds that gently sweep,

A fleeting beauty, in Jeju's soul so deep.

Lava tubes carve the earth, a hidden world below,

Mysteries in the darkness, where silent rivers flow.

Caves of wonder, nature's secret art,

Celebrating the City of Jeju

Jeju's veins, pulsing through its heart.

Dol hareubang stand, guardians of the isle,

Stone grandfathers with their eternal smile.

Silent watchers, through centuries they've seen,

The ebb and flow of life, in a land evergreen.

From the heart of Jeju, a song so pure and bright,

A melody of love, echoing through the night.

An ode to the island, in every verse and rhyme,

Jeju, eternal, transcending space and time.
Celebrating the City of
Jeju

ABOUT THE CREATOR

Walter the Educator is one of the pseudonyms for Walter Anderson. Formally educated in Chemistry, Business, and Education, he is an educator, an author, a diverse entrepreneur, and he is the son of a disabled war veteran. "Walter the Educator" shares his time between educating and creating. He holds interests and owns several creative projects that entertain, enlighten, enhance, and educate, hoping to inspire and motivate you. Follow, find new works, and stay up to date with Walter the Educator™

at WaltertheEducator.com

www.ingramcontent.com/pod-product-compliance
Lightning Source LLC
LaVergne TN
LVHW010622070526
838199LV00063BA/5229